CHILD LABOR IN AMERICA:
HISTORY, POLICY AND
LEGISLATIVE ISSUES

CHILD LABOR IN AMERICA: HISTORY, POLICY AND LEGISLATIVE ISSUES

WILLIAM G. WHITTAKER

Novinka Books
New York

Senior Editors: Susan Boriotti and Donna Dennis
Coordinating Editor: Tatiana Shohov
Office Manager: Annette Hellinger
Graphics: Wanda Serrano and Matt Dallow
Editorial Production: Maya Columbus, Alexis Klestov, Vladimir Klestov,
Matthew Kozlowski and Lorna Loperfido
Circulation: Ave Maria Gonzalez, Vera Popovic, Sean Corkery, Raymond Davis,
Melissa Diaz, Magdalena Nuñez, Marlene Nuñez and Jeannie Pappas
Communications and Acquisitions: Serge P. Shohov
Marketing: Cathy DeGregory

Library of Congress Cataloging-in-Publication Data
Available Upon Request

ISBN 1-59033-895-2.

Printed in the United States of America

CONTENTS

PREFACE

The history of child labor in America is long and, in some cases, unsavory. It dates back to the founding of the United States. Traditionally, most children, except for the privileged few, had always worked — either for their parents or for an outside employer. Through the years, child labor practices have changed — and so have the benefits and risks associated with employment of children. In some respects, altered workplace technology has served to make work easier and less hazardous. At the same time, some processes and equipment have rendered the workplace more dangerous — especially for the very young.

Child labor first became a federal legislative issue at least as far back as 1906 with the introduction of the Beveridge proposal for regulation of the types of work in which children might be engaged. Although the 1906 legislation was not adopted, it led to extended study of the conditions under which children were employed or allowed to work and to a series of legislative proposals — some approved, others defeated or overturned by the courts — culminating in the Fair Labor Standards Act (FLSA) of 1938. The latter statute, amended periodically, remains the primary federal law dealing with the employment of children.

Although providing a framework for regulation of child labor (and, in some cases, forbidding it entirely), the FLSA is not comprehensive, nor does it deal with all employment of children in precisely the same way. Generally speaking, work by young persons (under 18 years of age) in mines and factories is not allowed. What other types of work may be suitable (or especially hazardous) for persons under 18 years of age has been left to the discretion of the Secretary of Labor. Some types of work — for example, some newspaper sales and delivery, theatrical (and related) employment — fall beyond the scope of FLSA child labor requirements. Finally, a distinction has been made between employment in non-agricultural fields and in agriculture — and, in the latter case, between work for a parent or guardian in an agricultural setting and commercial employment.

In the 107th Congress, a range of child labor legislation has been introduced. Some proposals focus upon precise issues: "traveling sales crews," work by Amish youth (14 year olds) in wood processing plants, protection for young persons who might otherwise find themselves working in socially harmful environments. Other proposals deal more broadly with the general scope of child labor regulation — and, specifically, with child labor in agriculture.

In some cases, the issues have been frequently before the Congress or administratively before the Department of Labor. Thus far in the 107th Congress, no action has been taken on the various proposals related to employment of children.

Efforts to regulate (or to prohibit) certain forms of child labor in America largely commenced late in the 19th century — often at the state level. During the first decade of the 20th century, child labor became a federal concern. Congressional hearings were followed by extensive study of the issue — and by several abortive efforts to deal with child labor through law. Finally, with adoption of the Fair Labor Standards Act (1938), the modern federal role in child labor regulation took shape. But, debate concerning the issue has continued into the 107th Congress.[1]

Through the years, regulation of child labor has been contentious, sparking sharp differences of opinion. Some have urged modification of existing federal child labor restraints to afford greater opportunities for young persons to gain entry into the world of work — and to make their employment more convenient and profitable for employers. Others have questioned whether young children ought to be employed at all — especially while attending school. There would seem to be trade-offs, resting upon fundamental socio-economic philosophy and the value one places upon time. For example, when is child labor a healthy and useful introduction to the discipline of workplace? And, when might it divert young persons from academic work and/or place them at physical risk? Do children (however defined) need time for their own purposes; and, if so, how much time? How might one distinguish between freedom (to play, to think, to associate informally with peers) and idleness that may be conducive to activities that may be less wholesome than some types of work? Is some work *suitable* for

---

[1] This report is a brief introduction to child labor and related policy issues. For a more authoritative interpretation of the child labor requirements of the Fair Labor Standards Act, consult 29 CFR 570 ff.

young children (i.e., persons at various ages below 18 years of age) and, if so, how might *suitable work* be distinguished from work that is not suitable or that could be deemed to be "particularly hazardous" for persons under 18 years of age?

The history of child labor in American workplaces can be divided, roughly, into three periods. *First.* From the late 19th century to 1941, reformers sought to remove children from the workplace (whether factory, field, or tenement house) and to encourage more extended school attendance. *Second.* With World War II, the focus shifted to alleged labor shortages for war production. Some urged modification of work restrictions for older children: too young for the draft but old enough to be useful employees. *Third.* By the late 1940s, another shift took place. Too many older youths were believed to be out of school, out of work, and unable to find employment for which, it was argued, they were often unprepared both in terms of training and discipline. Thus, various "school-to-work" transition programs were developed together with "incentives" for employers to hire youth workers.

This book is intended as an brief introduction to the issue of child labor. It sketches the early history of child labor regulation and reviews certain recent federal initiatives in that area. Finally, it discusses currently pending child labor legislation.

Chapter 1

EARLY CHILD LABOR IN AMERICA

Prior to the late 19th century, employment of children largely reflected socio-economic class stratification. Where children were of working-class families, it was largely assumed that they would work — even when they were very young. Some were employed in the *street trades:* delivery of newspapers and telegrams, shining boots and shoes, running errands in various (often, unwholesome) sections of the city and at whatever hours the task demanded. Others were engaged in *industrial homework:* work often reserved for the very young who could work, usually alongside a parent or another adult, in a tenement flat in segments of garment production or in other types of work that could be performed, often on *a piece rate* basis, in one's place of residence. Still others worked in mines or factories: most notoriously, perhaps, the *breaker boys* in the coal mines, the child workers in the textile mills, and the helpers in the glass factories.

Agricultural labor by children seems always to have been in a category by itself. Usually, until the early 20th century, such work seems to have been on the family farm (whatever its size) or in an agricultural operation in the general vicinity of a youth's place of residence — though he (or she) might reside and work beyond the view and reach of a parent. Such work was no less hazardous — and no less arduous — than that of the streets or tenement or industrial labor. Indeed, in some respects, agricultural work may have been more dangerous.

Regulation of child labor has been motivated by diverse concerns: economic, humane, and more broadly social. In the 19th and early 20th centuries, child workers were often viewed as an alternative source of low-wage labor who vied with their parents and other adults for employment — even at the cost of their own health and education. Products of child labor competed with goods produced by adults, exerting a downward pressure on wages and living standards. Aside from health and safety hazards, inadequate rest, it was argued, left children ill-suited for educational activities and, in turn, as adults, ill-prepared for employment or for the support of their own children — thus, extending the cycle of poverty and adding to social-welfare costs.[2]

OPPOSITION TO CHILD LABOR BEGINS TO ORGANIZE

Through the latter half of the 19th century, the trade union movement developed strong opposition to child labor. New York labor activist Samuel Gompers championed child labor reform in New York state and later, as president of the American Federation of Labor (AFL), used his influence to improve the lot of working children.[3] Worker's advocate "Mother" (Mary Harris) Jones brought added visibility to the plight of child workers — and to that of their parents as well.[4] After its organization in 1899, the National Consumers League (NCL), under the leadership of Florence Kelley, took up the campaign against child labor as did a significant body of social workers, clergy, and concerned individuals.[5] In 1904, these forces were drawn

---

[2] There is an extensive Literature on child labor in America during the late 19th and early 20th centuries. See, for example: Clopper, Edward N. *Child Labor in the City Streets.* New York, The Macmillan Company, 1912; Lumpkin, Katharine DuPre, and Dorothy Wolff Douglas. *Child Workers in America.* New York, Robert M. McBride & Company, 1937; Markham, Edwin, Benjamin B. Lindsey, and George Creel. *Children In Bondage.* New York, Hearst's International Library Co., 1914; and Spargo, John. *The Bitter Cry of the Children.* New York, The Macmillan Company, 1906.

[3] Bremner, Robert H. *From the Depths: The Discovery of Poverty in the United States.* New York, New York University Press, 1964. p. 218, notes: "The labor unions had been active in the [child labor] movement since the days of the Knights of Labor in the 1880's, and Gompers only slightly exaggerated the facts when he declared [in 1906]: 'There is not a child labor law on the statute books of the United States but has been put there by the efforts of the trade-union movement.'" But, he added: "It is unlikely... that the campaign against child labor would have made such rapid headway after 1900 had it not been for the pressure brought to bear on both public opinion and legislatures by voluntary groups such as the consumers' leagues, state charities aid associations, federations of women's clubs, and the child-labor committees." See also: Gompers, Samuel. *Labor and the Common Welfare.* New York, E. P. Dutton & Company, 1919. p. 129; Felt, Jeremy P. *Hostages of Fortune: Child Labor Reform in New York State.* Syracuse, Syracuse University Press, 1965. p. 10-13, 60, and 196-197; and Walker, Roger W. The A.F.L. and Child-Labor Legislation: An Exercise in Frustration. *Labor History,* summer 1970. p. 323-340.

[4] Parton, Mary Field (ed.). *The Autobiography of Mother Jones.* Chicago, Charles H. Kerr Publishing Company, 1980. p. 71-83, 118-131.

[5] Concerning the work of the National Consumers' League, see: Goldmark, Josephine. *Impatient Crusader.* Urbana, University of Illinois Press, 1953, a biography of Florence Kelley; Sklar, Kathryn K. *Florence Kelley and the Nation's Work.* New Haven, Yale

together with the establishment of the National Child Labor Committee (NCLC) which, thereafter, would remain a central force in the movement to end the exploitation of children in the workplace.[6]

Child labor regulation generally commenced at the state level. Early laws were experimental, loosely drawn, and, where they exerted a restraining influence, subject to court challenge. Each type of work by children — in the mines, factories, fields, the street trades, etc. — presented its own special challenges for reformers; but, industrial homework by children was especially difficult to restrain. Although often not formally *employed*, children worked in tenement sweatshops making clothing, processing food, and engaging in whatever other work might profitably be conducted at home. Any tenement might become a little factory where conditions were adverse (often, effectively unregulated) and hours of work were unrestrained except by exhaustion. Thus, child labor and industrial homework, from a regulatory/reform perspective, became intermeshed. Reformers tended to agree that child labor could not be controlled while industrial homework continued: that regulation of the latter, *per se*, would never be successful. A total ban on the system was needed.[7]

Reformers, however, did not always agree on timing or overall strategy. Most seem to have concurred that, ultimately, reform would need to be federal. Faced with state regulation of child labor and/or industrial homework, employers could simply move to another state. Further, those who utilized child labor could play one jurisdiction against another in terms of wage-based economic development. For labor standards, it was a *race to the bottom*. At the same time, the strength of reform organization varied from one state to another. Some believed that state action was more nearly feasible than securing broader national change — at least for the present.

University Press, 1995; and Storrs, Landon R. Y. *Civilizing Capitalism: The National Consumers' League, Women's Activism, and Labor Standards in the New Deal Era*. Chapel Hill, University of North Carolina Press, 2000. (Hereafter cited as Storrs, *Civilizing Capitalism*).

[6] Trattner, Walter I. *Crusade for the Children: A History of the National Child Labor Committee and Child Labor Reform in America*. Chicago, Quadrangle Books, 1970. (Hereafter cited as Trattner, *Crusade for the Children*).

[7] Shallcross, Ruth E. *Industrial Homework: An Analysis of Homework Regulations, Here and Abroad*. New York, Industrial Affairs Publishing Co., 1939; Boris, Eileen. *Home to Work: Motherhood and the Politics of Industrial Homework in the United States*. New York, Cambridge University Press, 1994; and Crawford, Ruth. Development and Control of Industrial Homework. *Monthly Labor Review*, June 1944. p. 1145-1158.

THE EARLY FEDERAL ROLE IN
CHILD LABOR REGULATION

In 1906, Senator Albert Beveridge (R-Ind.) and Representative Herbert Parsons (R-N. Y.) introduced legislation to prevent employment of children in factories and mines. Debate on this first federal initiative continued through several years but did not become law. However, the proposal, with the work of the various reform groups, raised the visibility of child labor as a public policy issue.[8] In 1907, legislation was approved (P.L. 59-41) which authorized the Secretary of Commerce and Labor (then, a single department) "to investigate and report upon the industrial, social, moral, education, and physical condition of woman and child workers in the United States." The result was a detailed survey which appeared in 19 volumes between 1910 and 1913.[9] Building from that evidentiary record, Congress turned again to the legislative process in an attempt to deal with child labor and related problems.

The Child Labor Initiatives (1916-1924)

Although Congress and the advocates of reform sought to limit exploitive/oppressive child labor, the best approach was not immediately clear. Thus, sequentially, Congress moved in three directions — each, uniformly unsuccessful.

In 1916, a decade after the Beveridge proposal, new federal child labor legislation was introduced by Senator Robert Owen (D-Okla.) and by Representative Edward Keating (D-Colo.) with support from the reform community. A regional struggle then in progress pitted one state against another in a contest for economic growth with low-wage non-union labor a bargaining chip. Southern manufacturers viewed child labor restriction as an "effort of northern agitators to kill the infant industries of the south."[10] The *Owen-Keating Act (1916),* based on the commerce clause of the

---

[8]   Braeman, John. Albert J. Beveridge and the First National Child Labor Bill. *Indiana Magazine of History*, March 1964. p. 1-36.

[9]   U.S. Congress. Senate. 61st Cong., 2nd Sess., Document No. 645. *Report on Condition of Woman and Child Wage-Earners in the United States.* 19 Volumes. Washington, U.S. Govt. Print. Off., 1913. See also: U.S. Department of Labor. Bureau of Labor Statistics. Women in Industry Series No. 5. *Summary of the Report on Condition of Woman and Child Wage Earners in the United States.* Washington, Govt. Print. Off., 1916. 445 p.

[10] Abbott, Grace. Federal Regulation of Child Labor, 1906-38. *The Social Service Review,* September 1939. p. 411. (Hereafter cited as Abbott, *Federal Regulation of Child Labor).*

Constitution, sought to ban movement in interstate commerce of certain products of child labor. In June 1918, however, the Supreme Court declared the Act unconstitutional (*Hammer v. Dagenhart*, 247 U.S. 251), and reformers searched for a new approach.[11]

Congress next turned to the taxing power as an indirect method for controlling child labor. Senator Atlee Pomerene (D-Ohio) proposed to levy a 10% tax "on the annual net profits of industries" that employed children in violation of certain age and hours standards.[12] The tax penalty would offset any competitive advantage that child labor might otherwise provide. Although the measure was in reality child labor legislation, it was hoped that it might secure Court approval. The Supreme Court demurred and the *Pomerene (child labor tax) Act (1919)* was declared unconstitutional in May 1922 (*Bailey v. Drexel Furniture Company*, 259 U.S. 20).[13]

In the wake of the *Drexel* case, Samuel Gompers met at AFL headquarters with Florence Kelley of the National Consumers League, representatives of the NCLC, and others. After extended discussion and weighing of options, the group developed a proposal for a constitutional amendment to grant Congress the right "to limit, regulate, and prohibit the labor of persons under 18 years of age." The *child labor amendment (1924)* involved far more than the mere passing of legislation since the case for approval had to be made to each state legislature. While the proponents of child labor reform began optimistically, support began to erode on a number of fronts for reasons not necessarily associated with child labor per *se*. The proposed amendment remained unratified in 1937 when Congress turned back to direct legislation with consideration of the Fair Labor Standards Act.[14]

---

[11] Trattner, *Crusade for the Children,* p. 119-138. See also: Keating, Edward. *The Gentleman from Colorado: A Memoir.* Denver, Sage Books, 1964. p. 349-355; Berger, Lawrence R., and S. Ryan Johannson. Child Health in the Workplace: The supreme Court in *Hammer v. Dagenhart* (1918). *Journal of Health Politics, Policy and Law,* spring 1980. p. 81-97; Lea, Arden J. Cotton Textiles and the Federal Child Labor Act of 1916. *Labor History,* fall 1975. p. 485-494; and Trattner, Walter I. The First Federal Child Labor Law (1916). *Social Science Quarterly,* December 1969. p. 507-524.

[12] Abbott, *Federal Regulation of Child Labor*, p. 416.

[13] Trattner, *Crusade for the Children*, p. 138-142.

[14] Ibid., p. 163-186. See also: Now the States Must Act! The Past, the Present and the Future of the Effort to Free American Childhood. *American Federationist,* July 1924. p. 541-553 — the AFL journal of which Gompers was editor; McQuade, Vincent A. *The American Catholic Attitude on Child Labor Since 1891.* Washington, The Catholic University of America, 1938. p. 79-100, 112-128; and Greene, Thomas R. The Catholic Committee for the Ratification of the Child Labor Amendment, 1935-1937: Origin and Limits. *The Catholic Historical Review,* April 1988. p. 248-269.

Early New Deal Enactments (1933-1937)

From the period of the Beveridge bill (1906) to the New Deal era, children's advocates remained divided over the means for ending exploitive child labor. The reform community initially split with respect to federal action. Then, it had largely coalesced behind the Owen-Keating (1916) and Pomerene (1918) bills, debating long and hard over the wisdom of a constitutional amendment (1924). By late 1932, leaders of the Children's Bureau in the Department of Labor (DOL) and the NCLC, with others, decided to shift their focus away from ratification of the constitutional amendment (which was then perceived to be in doubt) and back toward action by individual states.

In retrospect, this shift of emphasis may have been a misreading of the times. "By 1933," notes Walter Trattner in his reform-oriented study, *Crusade for the Children*, "the spreading contagion of child labor had found every weakness and loophole in state labor legislation." He observes: "Sweatshops and fly-by-night plants were exploiting children for little or no pay, moving at will across state lines to take advantage of laws of nearby states. The individual states were unable to halt these abuses which had far-reaching effects, including the complete breakdown of wage scales." Thus, in competitive terms, some argued, it wasn't feasible for individual states to lead in labor-related reform, even were they predisposed to do so. Trattner concludes: "Everywhere people were looking to Washington for help and direction."[15]

Soon after the inauguration of President Roosevelt, Congress passed the National Industrial Recovery Act (NIRA, 1933). Under the National Recovery Administration (NRA), industries were encouraged to develop codes of fair competition, which in many instances came to include minimum wage and overtime pay standards, a ban on industrial homework, and the restriction or elimination of child labor. Elimination of child labor under the Cotton Textile Code seemed, momentarily, a major breakthrough. However, in May 1935, the NIRA was declared unconstitutional (*Schechter Poultry Corp. et al v. United States*, 295 U.S. 495).[16]

The Agricultural Adjustment Act (AAA) of May 1933 and the Jones-Costigan Sugar Stabilization Act (1934) were roughly companion measures

---

[15] Trattner, *Crusade for the Children*, p. 189. See also: Yellowitz, Irwin. The Origins of Unemployment Reform. *Labor History*, fall 1968. p. 354-355.

[16] Schoenfeld, Margaret H. Analysis of the Labor Provisions of the N.R.A. Codes. *Monthly Labor Review*, March 1935. p. 591-595; Merritt, Ella Arvilla. Trend of Child Labor, 1927-1936. *Monthly Labor Review*, December 1937. p. 1371-1390.

to the NIRA. In exchange for certain price supports, the government required grower/producer adherence to certain labor and marketing standards.[17] In 1937, the AAA was similarly declared unconstitutional.

In an effort to salvage NIRA and AAA labor standards, less comprehensive measures followed. *First.* Labor Secretary Frances Perkins, long a child labor reformer, urged that government, *as a consumer* (a more likely constitutional strategy), refuse to purchase items produced by child labor or under unsafe and unclean conditions in tenements (industrial homework). These restrictions were made part of the Public Contracts Act (1936), co-sponsored by Senator David Walsh (D-Mass.) and Representative Arthur Healey (D-Mass.) — i.e., the Walsh-Healey Act.[18] *Second.* Agricultural labor standards, though limited, reemerged in the Beet Sugar Act (1937), again linked to a federal support system.[19]

The FLSA and General Child Labor Regulation (1938)

Following adoption of Walsh-Healey, Secretary Perkins urged passage of general federal minimum wage and overtime pay legislation. Trattner noted that Roosevelt, possibly believing that the wage/hour measure could more easily be enacted "if it were made more attractive by integrating it with child labor," combined the several provisions.[20] Perkins recalls that child labor provisions were added, late in the process, at the urging of Grace Abbott, for many years head of the Children's Bureau at DOL. "The President readily agreed and was delighted that we might make this bill cover child labor as well as low wages and long hours."[21] After exhaustive debate, the Fair Labor Standards Act (FLSA), with its child labor provisions, became law during the summer of 1938.[22]

---

[17] Trattner, *Crusade for the Children*, p. 209-210; Greenbaum, Fred. *Fighting Progressive: A Biography of Edward P. Costigan.* Washington, Public Affairs Press, 1971. p. 143-154; and, Jamieson, Stuart. *Labor Unionism in American Agriculture.* Washington, U.S. Department of Agriculture, Bulletin No. 836, June 1945. p. 243-244.

[18] Morton, Herbert C. *Public Contracts and Private Wages: experience Under the Walsh-Healey Act.* Washington, the Brookings Institution, 1965. p. 14-15, 23-24. Where government efforts to regulate private sector labor standards had often been disallowed by the courts, setting standards for itself as a consumer had been more successful.

[19] Concerning constitutional issues of this period, see: Chambers, John W. The Big Switch: Justice Roberts and the Minimum-Wage Cases. *Labor History*, winter 1969. p. 44-73.

[20] Trattner, *Crusade for the Children*, p. 203. See also Storrs, *Civilizing Capitalism*, p. 334.

[21] Perkins, Frances. *The Roosevelt I Knew.* New York, The Viking Press, 1946. p. 257.

[22] Although child labor concerns were voiced during debate on the wage/hour legislation, separate hearings were held on that issue. See U.S. Congress. Senate. Committee on

The FLSA was not a complete victory for advocates of child labor regulation. Historian Jeremy Felt argues that the Act may have served "as a deterrent and as an educational force" but adds that "in those areas where children are useful they continue to be employed."[23] Further, the Act did not deal with competition from goods produced abroad by child workers under conditions the FLSA proscribed in America.

During the early 1940s, as enforcement of the FLSA commenced, DOL found (like reformers early in the century) that illegal exploitation of children as laborers was extremely difficult to eradicate where industrial homework persisted. Attempts to regulate the latter were unproductive. By the mid-1940s, DOL had imposed an outright ban on industrial homework in certain garment-related fields. Thereafter, abusive child labor seems to have faded as a public policy issue, gradually being replaced by concern with youth unemployment, training, and "school-to-work" transition.

Interstate Commerce. *To Regulate the Products of Child Labor.* 75thCong., 1st Sess., May 12, 18, and 20, 1937. 192 p.

[23] Felt, Jeremy P. The child Labor Provisions of the Fair Labor Standards Act. *Labor History,* fall 1970. P. 4478-479. Jonathan Grossman, then DOL staff historian, similarly notes: "The law avoided some sectors of the work force where most abuses of child labor were concentrated, such as migrant labor, and 'street trades,' such as newspaper venders and shoeshine boys. According to one estimate, only 30,000 child laborers outside of agriculture would be affected." See Grossman, Jonathan. Fair Labor standards Act of 1938: Maximum Struggle for a Minimum Wage. *Monthly Labor Review,* June 1978. P. 29.

Chapter 2

CHILD LABOR UNDER THE
FAIR LABOR STANDARDS ACT

The FLSA (1938, as amended) protects children by setting conditions under which they may be employed and, in certain types of work, prohibiting their employment altogether.[24] While the basic structure of the Act has changed little since 1938, Congress has altered specific provisions of the statute and DOL has variously refined its administration through the rulemaking process.

THE BASIC PATTERN OF COVERAGE

Under the FLSA, employers may not use "oppressive child labor in commerce or in the production of goods for commerce." "Oppressive" is partially defined in the Act and partly left to the discretion of the Secretary. Persons under 18 years of age may not be employed in mining or manufacturing or "in any occupation which the Secretary of Labor shall... declare to be *particularly hazardous* for the employment of children... or detrimental to their health or well-being." (Italics added.) Otherwise, 16

---

[24] Section 203(I) defines "oppressive child labor." Section 212 defines the relationship of goods produced by child labor with movement in interstate commerce. Section 213(c) sets forth the specialized treatment of child workers under the Act and the pattern of exemptions from otherwise standard coverage. The states may (and normally do) have their own child labor laws. While these may supplement the FLSA, they are not necessarily consistent with the FLSA standard. Where there is overlapping coverage, the higher standard (most protective of the youth worker) will normally prevail. When exploring coverage in any particular case, both the state and federal statutes need to be taken into account.

years of age is the usual minimum age for employment. The Secretary may permit employment of persons 14 to 16 years of age in work not deemed "oppressive," that does not interfere with the youth's schooling, and that is not detrimental to his/her "health and well-being." The Secretary has established hours during which children of various ages may work: i.e., the number of hours they may be employed, taking into account the demands of academic attendance.

EXEMPTIONS

The Fair Labor Standards Act is a broad umbrella statute that sets forth general policies and, at the same time, may specify in precise detail — either in the statute *per se* or through implementing regulations — how coverage is to be applied: i.e., who is covered and who is exempt. Because of the technical nature of wage/hour and child labor law, it may be unwise to accept any segment of the statute (or regulations) in isolation and at face value. Most provisions of the Act have either been the subject of litigation or have long administrative/legislative histories. What may seem obvious on the surface may, in fact, be inordinately complex.[25]

The FLSA, rooted in the commerce clause of the Constitution, excludes from coverage children who are not involved in activities affecting interstate commerce — *though such persons may be protected by state statutes.* Also excluded are children employed by "a parent or a person standing in place of a parent employing his own child or a child in his custody." A child, for instance, assisting a parent (helping around a "mom-and-pop" corner grocery or doing chores around the home) would not be covered under federal child labor law. Nor do the child labor provisions of the Act apply to children employed as actors or in related activities. Traditionally, the "street trades" (e.g., newspaper delivery) have been regarded as appropriate for children and, thus, are not restrained by FLSA child labor provisions. During the mid-1990s, the Departmental regulations were altered, administratively, to allow youth of 14 and 15 years of age to work in certain "sports-attending services at professional sporting events."

---

[25] *See Title 29 CFR, Part 570 ff., for a more complete explanation of child labor regulation in general.* In addition, DOL may have issued "opinion letters" that apply a provision of the FLSA to specific workplaces.

Table 1. Summary of Child Labor Regulation
under the Fair Labor Standards Act

Non-agricultural jobs	Agricultural employment
Regulations governing youth employment in non-form jobs differ somewhat from those pertaining to agricultural employment. In non-farm work, the permissible jobs and hours of work, by age, are as follows:	In farm work, permissible jobs and hours of work by age, are as follows:
(1) Youths 18 years or older may perform any job, whether hazardous or not, for unlimited hours;	(1) Youths 16 years and older may perform any job, whether hazardous or not, for unlimited hours;
(2) Youths 16 and 17 years old may perform any nonhazardous job, for unlimited hours; and	(2) Youths 14 and 15 years old may perform any nonhazardous farm job outside of school hours;
(3) Youths 14 and 15 years old may work outside school hours in various non-manufacturing, non-mining, nonhazardous jobs under the following conditions: no more than 3 hours on a school day, 18 hours in a school week, 8 hours on a non-school day, or 40 hours in a non-school week. Also, work may not begin before 7 a.m., nor end after 7 p.m., except from June 1 through Labor Day, when evening hours are extended to 9 p.m.	(3) Youths 12 and 13 years old may work outside of school hours in nonhazardous jobs, either with a parent's written consent or on the same farm as the parent(s);
Fourteen is the minimum age for most non-farm work. However, at any age, youth may deliver newspapers; perform in radio, television, movie, or theatrical productions; work for parents in their sole-owned non-farm business (except in manufacturing or on hazardous jobs); or, gather evergreens and make evergreen wreaths.	(4) Youths under 12 years old may perform jobs on farms owned or operated by parent(s), or with a parent's written consent, outside of school hours in nonhazardous jobs on farms not covered by minimum wage requirements.*

* The "not covered by minimum wage" provision limits the exemption, effectively, to small farms. Children are allowed to perform *chores* for their parents on family farms and, at any age, to assist their parents.

Source: Material in this table has been excerpted from the *Handy Reference Guide to the Fair Labor Standards Act,* published by the U.S. Department of Labor, Employment Standards Administration, Wage and Hour Division, WH Publication 1282, Revised October 1996. *This summary is not all-inclusive.* See Title 29 CFR, Part 570 ff., for a more complete explanation of child labor regulation.

Child/youth employment in agriculture is treated somewhat differently from non-agricultural employment.[26] For example, a child working for a

---

[26] The Department of Labor *estimates* that, during the late 1990s, about 7% of all farmworkers were between 14 and 17 years of age: i.e., about 126,000 children in that age group were

parent on a family farm would not be covered under the FLSA. There are also disparities of treatment with respect to age and the types of work that children may perform. (See **Table 1** for a very general summary of these requirements.) Under the 1977 amendments to the Act, a specialized exemption, carefully circumscribed, was written into the statute for the employment of children of 10 and 11 years of age as hand harvest workers in agriculture.[27]

ENFORCEMENT

Even where child labor is banned, enforcement has been (and remains) difficult. FLSA compliance staff is relatively small and enforcement is often *complaint driven.* Child workers, themselves, are not likely to complain. If one assumes that children are employed with parental knowledge and/or consent, complaints from their family may not be frequent — even where such employment may be illegal and/or hazardous to the child. Where migratory agricultural work is concerned, enforcement problems are more complex.

Children, like adults, work for diverse reasons. Peer pressure may encourage young persons to seek employment. There may also be the desire for otherwise unaffordable consumer goods. But, they may also enter the workforce under pressure from parents who believe that employment, even for young children, provides good discipline and keeps youngsters off the street and out of mischief. A traditional argument for child labor has been economic necessity: i.e., contributing to total family income. If child workers and their parents fail to cooperate in enforcement of child labor law, then DOL compliance activity can become extremely difficult.

Some have urged non-parental oversight. If a child is having difficulty in school or is frequently truant, employment might be the cause. But, do school authorities have the time and resources to monitor the work arrangements of their students? When physicians treat young persons for

---

employed on American farms. However, an unknown number of youth younger than 14 years of age are also employed in agriculture. See U.S. Department of Labor. *Report on the Youth Labor Force.* Updated November 2000, p. 52-53.

[27] As the 1977 FLSA amendments were written, a grower could employ children age 10 and 11 so long as the grower/employer could demonstrate that any pesticides used in the production process would not be harmful for children under 12. Since growers have not been able to demonstrate the harmlessness of such pesticides, etc., they have the choice of (a) not using pesticides or (b) not employing children age 10 or 11. Children 12 years of age can be employed.

problems that might be work-related, can they reasonably be expected to contact the child/patient's employer and inspect conditions in the workplace? Efforts in these directions, early in the century, were often unsuccessful but systems of work permits — sometimes linking school attendance and performance to employment — continue to be urged, together with work injury reporting.

HAZARDOUS OCCUPATIONS ORDERS

By definition, under the FLSA, manufacturing and mining work is deemed too hazardous *for persons under 18 years of age*. However, the Secretary may, at his or her discretion (normally through the rulemaking procedure), designate other types of work as similarly too hazardous for persons under 18. In such cases, the Secretary will issue "hazardous occupations orders" or HOs which are incorporated in the Code of Federal Regulations (see **Table 2**).

Often, an exception will be made (and written into the HO) with respect to apprentices and student-learners. The regulations make clear that, where there is a conflict between the HOs and any other provision of law, the higher standard prevails. Each HO is precise, frequently responding to problems that have arisen in the workplace. Currently, there are 17 specific HOs in place with respect to non-agricultural employment which include (among others) occupations such as work involving "manufacturing or storing explosives," "operation of power-driven meat-processing machines and occupations involving slaughtering, meat packing or processing, or rendering," and "logging occupations and occupations in the operation of any sawmill, lath mill, shingle mill, or cooperage stock mill."[28] Eleven others have been published with respect to agricultural employment (see **Table 3**). Changes in the HOs or HOAs often invoke close oversight by the Congress.

---

[28]   See 29 CFR 570.50 ff.

Table 2. Hazardous Occupations Orders Issued by the Secretary of Labor: Work Generally Unsuitable for Certain Young Persons

HO 1 (29 CFR 570.51)	Occupations in or about plants or establishments manufacturing or storing explosives or articles containing explosive components.
HO 2 (29 CFR 570.52)	Occupations of motor-vehicle driver and outside helper.
HO 3 (29 CFR 570.53)	Coal mine occupations.
HO 4 (29 CFR 570.54)	Logging occupations and occupations in the operation of any sawmill, lath mill, shingle mill, or cooperage stock mill.
HO 5 (29 CFR 570.55)	Occupations involved in the operation of power-driven wood-working machines.
HO 6 (29 CFR 570.56)	Exposure to radioactive substances and to ionizing radiations.
HO 7 (29 CFR 570.58)	Occupations involved in the operation of power-driven hoisting apparatus.
HO 8 (29 CFR 570.59)	Occupations involved in the operations of power-driven metal forming, punching, and shearing machines.
HO 9 (29 CFR 570.60)	Occupations in connection with mining, other than coal.
HO 10 (29 CFR 570.61)	Occupations in the operation of power-driven meat-processing machines and occupations involving slaughtering, meat packing or processing, or rendering.
HO 11 (29 CFR 570.62)	Occupations involved in the operation of bakery machines.
HO 12 (29 CFR 570.63)	Occupations involved in the operation of paper-products machines.
HO 13 (29 CFR 570.64)	Occupations involved in the manufacture of brick, tile, and kindred products.
HO 14 (29 CFR 570.65)	Occupations involved in the operations of circular saws, band saws, and guillotine shears.
HO 15 (29 CFR 570.66)	Occupations involved in wrecking, demolition, and shipbreaking operations.
HO 16 (29 CFR 570.67)	Occupations in roofing operations.
HO 17 (29 CFR 570.68)	Occupations in excavation operations.

Note: Each of these Hazardous Occupation Orders is developed in detail in the Code of Federal Regulations with specific qualifying factors explained.

Table 3. Hazardous Occupations Orders Issued by the Secretary of Labor: Work Unsuitable for Young Persons under 16 Years of Age Employed in Agriculture

HOA 1   Operating a tractor of over 20 PTO horsepower, or connecting or disconnecting an implement or any of its parts to or from such a tractor.

HOA 2   Operating or assisting to operate (including starting, stopping, adjusting, feeding, or any other activity involving physical contact associated with the operation) any of the following machines:
  – Corn picker, cotton picker, grain combine, hay mower, forage harvester, hay baler, potato differ, or mobile pea viner;
  – Feed grinder, crop dryer, forage blower, auger conveyor, or the unloading mechanism of a nongravity-type self-unloading wagon or trailer; or
  – Power post-hole differ, power post driver, or nonwalking type rotary tiller.

HOA 3   Operating or assisting to operate (including starting, stopping, adjusting, feeding, or any other activity involving physical contact associated with the operation) any of the following machines:
  – Trencher or earthmoving equipment;
  – Fork lift;
  – Potato combine; or
  – Power-driven circular, band, or chain saw.

HOA 4   Working on a farm in a yard, pen, or stall occupied by a:
  – Bull, boar, or stud horse maintained for breeding purposes; or
  – Sow with suckling pigs, or cow with newborn calf (with umbilical cord present).

HOA 5   Felling, bucking, skidding, loading, or unloading timber with butt diameter of more than 6 inches.

HOA 6   Working from a ladder or scaffold (painting, repairing, or building structures, pruning trees, picking fruit, etc.) At a height of over 20 feet

HOA 7   Driving a bus, truck, or automobile when transporting passengers, or riding on a tractor as a passenger or helper.

HOA 8   Working inside:
  – A fruit, forage, or grain storage designed to retain an oxygen deficient or toxic atmosphere;
  – An upright silo within 2 weeks after silage has been added or when a top unloading device is in operating position;
  – A manure pit; or
  – A horizontal silo while operating a tractor for packing purposes.

HOA 9   Handling or applying (including cleaning or decontaminating equipment, disposal or return of empty containers, or serving as a flagman for aircraft applying) agricultural chemicals classified... as Category I of toxicity, identified by the word "poison" and the "skull and crossbones" on the label; or a Category II of toxicity, identified by the word "warning" on the label.

HOA 10   Handing or using a blasting agent, including but not limited to, dynamite, black powder, sensitized ammonium nitrate, blasting caps, and primer cord.

HOA 11   Transporting, transferring, or applying anhydrous ammonia.

Source: 29 CFR 570-71.

Chapter 3

RE-EMERGENCE OF THE CHILD LABOR ISSUE (1982-2000)

By the late 1940s, exploitation and endangerment of young children in the world of work was popularly believed to have been resolved through legislation (the FLSA) and through the administrative discretion of the Secretary of Labor in implementing the FLSA. But, occasionally, someone would recall that very young children still toiled in field harvest work or an especially egregious accident would bring the more general issue back to the front page.

At the same time, there had begun a gradual shift of focus: to a *new* issue i.e., inadequate opportunities for youth employment — and the related question of delinquency. In May 1961, for example, some 500 men and women met in Washington "to discuss [this]... serious but little known national problem." The summary report of the conference observed:

> Again and again in the past decade, juvenile delinquency and the outbreaks of youthful street gangs have made headlines. The fact that large numbers of our youth, 16 to 21 years of age, are out of school and unemployed, significant as it may be in terms of delinquency, has far greater significance in terms of what changes are taking place in our society... .

The summary report pointed to an unemployment rate of 17.1% for this age group — with a somewhat higher rate for minority youth. "There have always been young people who dropped out before finishing high school or grade school... . But until recently, except during the depression, there were ample-unskilled jobs for workers of limited education." That, the report stated, was no longer true. "When no work is to be had at home, the small-town boys and the farm boys go off to the cities where, ill-prepared for urban jobs, they swell the ranks of the young unemployed." And that, argued Harvard's James B. Conant, "is *social dynamite.*"[29]

Through the next 2 decades, the literature on youth employment (youth joblessness) grew rapidly with numerous panaceas for the *problem* being advanced. In retrospect, there seems to have been little agreement among policy analysts — except that the problem was serious.[30]

Whatever the impact of youth employment (or joblessness) may be, large numbers of youths have continued to seek and to find work (see **Table 4**). Although many young persons are employed while less than 15 years of age, surveys have only commenced to assess their work patterns.[31] Consideration of employment of those 15 years old and over has long been a part of the analytical work of the Bureau of Labor Statistics and is better understood.

---

[29] National Committee for Children and Youth. *Social Dynamite: The Report of the Conference on Unemployed, Out-of-School Youth in Urban Areas, May 24-26, 1961.* Washington, 1961. p. 1-2. Italics in original.

[30] The article, "To Be Young, Black and Out of Work," *The New York Times Magazine,* October 23, 1977, p. 39, stated: "Nearly half of all minority youths between 16 and 19 who are in the work force are unemployed." Similarly, *The AFL-CIO American Federationist,* January 1978, p. 1, in an article by Barbara Becnel, "Black Workers: Progress Derailed," observed that unemployment rates "for black teenagers have reached catastrophic levels. In 1976 they averaged 39.2 percent, and in July 1977 they reached an all-time recorded high of 45.5 percent." See: U.S. Congress. Joint Economic Committee. Hearing. *Youth Unemployment.* 94th Cong., 2nd Sess., September 9, 1976. Washington, Govt. Print. Off., 1977, 130 p.; and U.S. Congress. Senate. Committee on the Budget. Hearing. *Youth Unemployment.* 95th Cong., 2nd Sess., February 17, 1978. Washington, Govt. Print. Off., 1978. 136 p.

[31] Concerning employment of workers under 15 years of age, see the collection of essays on youth employment, based on the National Longitudinal Surveys Program of the Bureau of Labor Statistics commencing from 1997 (NLSY97), published in the August 2001 edition of the *Monthly Labor Review.* In their article, "Illegal Child Labor in the United States: Prevalence and Characteristics" *(Industrial and Labor Relations Review,* October 2000, p. 17-40), Douglas L. Kruse and Douglas Mahony examine this sub-set of youth workers and evaluate the value of currently available data on workers under 15 years of age.

Table 4. Employed Persons 15 to 17 Years of Age by Class of Worker, Selected Characteristics, School and Summer Months, 1996-1998

Sex, age, race, & Hispanic origin[b]	School months			Summer months		
	Total employed (in thsds)	Percent distribution[a]		Total employed (in thsds)	Percent distribution[a]	
		Wage & salary workers	Self-employed workers[c]		Wage & salary workers	Self-employed workers[c]
Total, 15-17 years	2,896	97.1	2.3	3,969	95.9	3.3
Male	1,460	96.3	2.9	2,070	94.7	4.3
Female	1,437	97.8	1.8	1,899	97.2	2.2
Age 15	366	92.3	6.3	694	90.3	8.2
Age 16	1,011	97.2	2.2	1,412	96.0	3.0
Age 17	1,520	98.1	1.4	1,862	97.9	1.6
White, 15-17 years	2,569	97.0	2.4	3,474	95.7	3.5
Black, 15-17 years	240	98.8	1.3	376	98.4	1.6
Hispanic origin, 15-17 years	225	97.3	1.8	309	96.8	1.6

[a] Percentages may not add up to 100% because unpaid family workers are not included here. There may also be some impact from rounding.

[b] Identification of youth by race and ethnicity may result in some double counting.

[c] Self-employed workers are those who work in their own business, trade, or profession and not for a regular employer: for example, mowing lawns, baby sitting, etc.

Source: The table is adapted from data provided in the *Report on the Youth Labor Force*, published by the U.S. Department of Labor, and updated November 2000, p. 43. Data are pooled (i.e., combined to increase the sample size) across a 3-year period.

Looking at labor force participation by 15 to 17 year old youth through the period 1996-1998, on average, "about a fourth of both male and female youths were employed during average school months. During the summer, about one-third of both male and female youths worked," the Department of Labor reported. But DOL also reported significant variations in employment status when considered in terms of race and ethnicity. About 28% of white youths were employed during school months; about 38% during the summer. For blacks, the comparable figures were 13% (school months) and 20% (summer); for youth of Hispanic origin, 15% (school months), 20% (summer).[32]

---

[32] U.S. Department of Labor. *Report on the Youth Labor Force.* Updated November 2000, p. 30-31. Hispanics are included in both black and white data sets. Data are pooled across a 3-year period.

THE REAGAN ERA INITIATIVES

In July 1982, Labor Secretary Raymond Donovan (for the Reagan Administration) proposed that existing child labor policy be updated. The Administration's plan would have: (a) opened more opportunities for employment for children of 14 and 15 years of age; (b) extended the number of hours per day and per week that such persons might be employed; (c) revised standards for the employment of child workers in jobs once considered too hazardous; and (d) simplified and broadened the manner in which employers could become certified by DOL to employ full-time students at less than the standard minimum wage.

The Donovan proposal sparked an immediate reaction. When opening hearings before the House Labor Standards Subcommittee of which he was chair, Representative George Miller (D-Calif.) sharply criticized the Administration's proposals.[33] In turn, Wage/Hour Administrator William Otter defended them as sound and reasonable public policy. He read from letters from young persons, parents and potential employers urging flexibility in child labor regulation so that 14 and 15 year olds could be more easily employed. Although acknowledging a high unemployment rate among 16 to 19 year olds, Otter affirmed his concern "about the unemployment levels of all age groups" and stated the view that "[u]nreasonable and artificial impediments to the employment of all age groups should be eliminated."[34]

Proponents and critics seemed to agree that the Reagan Administration "had walked into a minefield" where the child labor issue was concerned.[35] In February 1983, *Nation's Restaurant News* reported that "Federal wage and hour regulators are sifting through a blizzard of letters from restaurant operators across the nation supporting the Reagan Administration's plan to relax child labor restrictions on the employment of young teenagers in food-service outlets." But, the *News* also reported that the proposal had "generated a storm of protest from educational groups, labor unions and Congressmen who expressed outrage over what some described as a scheme to enable restauranteurs to exploit school age workers."[36]

---

[33] Press release from Congressman George Miller, July 27, 1982.
[34] U.S. Congress. House. Subcommittee on Labor Standards. Committee on Education and Labor. Hearings. *Oversight Hearings — Proposed Changes in Child Labor Regulations.* 97th Cong., 2nd Sess., July 28, and August 3, 1982. p. 1-30.
[35] Edelman, Peter. Child Labor Revisited. *The Nation*, August 21-28, 1982. p. 136.
[36] *Nation's Restaurant News*, February 28, 1983. p. 2.

For a time, the regulations remained under review with periodical speculation that their release was imminent. In late 1984, the *Nation's Restaurant News* reported that the proposal was "likely to resurface."[37] Later, it was speculated that they would likely appear "by the end of the year."[38] And after a year, it was noted that DOL was again delaying "action on a regulation governing the employment of minors between the ages of 14 and 16."[39] Some suggested "a politically inspired delay" in release of a final rule.[40] Whatever the cause, a final revision never appeared.

CONTROVERSIES AND CHANGES OF LAW

As the Reagan Administration proposals receded every further into the background, several committees of the Congress conducted hearings on aspects of child labor — a process that would continue, intermittently, through the 1980s and 1990s. But, although they established an evidentiary record, no general legislation restructuring child labor law was approved.

In 1987, Labor Secretary William Brock announced formation of a Child Labor Advisory Committee to assist him with interpretation of child labor issues. The Committee was chaired by Linda Golodner who was also executive director of the National Consumers' League. The advisory body quickly concluded that child labor was "often on the low end of the priority list" at DOL and that it took "very, very long for [its]... recommendations to get through the bureaucracy." In the spring of 1989, the Department explained that the suggestions of the Committee had, gradually, moved through four lower levels of review and that, by mid-May, they had reached the desk of the Administrator of the Wage and Hour Division.[41]

DOL is a large agency with diverse responsibilities. The new Bush Administration personnel, it can be reasonably assumed, would require at least a brief period during which to become acquainted with its operation and with their own new responsibilities. With the appointment of Elizabeth Dole

---

[37] Rankin, Ken. Pols May Pull Child Labor Scheme off Back Burner. *Nation's Restaurant News*, November 26, 1984. p. 9.

[38] Bureau of National Affairs. *Daily Labor Report*, April 23, 1984. p. A7.

[39] Bureau of National Affairs. *Daily Labor Report*, April 30, 1985. p. A9.

[40] Walsh, Joseph A. Teen-Age Work Rules Targeted Again. *UA Journal,* September 1982. p. 4.

[41] Bureau of National Affairs. *Daily Labor Report*, May 18, 1989. p. A10-A11. The Committee had addressed such issues as "door-to-door" sales by persons 14 to 15 years of age, a special overtime exemption for "bat boys," and work around commercial paper balers. It also examined the structure of penalties for child labor violations. During this period, GAO was looking into some of these same issues while the National Consumers' League launched its own independent review of child labor practices.

as Secretary of Labor (January 1989), the Department appears to have developed a more active interest in the welfare of working children. In mid-1989, the Secretary recruited William Brooks of General Motors to serve as Assistant Secretary for Employment Standards and charged him, *inter alia,* with child labor issues.[42]

Almost at once, the new assistant secretary was confronted with a GAO report affirming that child labor violations had increased dramatically during recent years. But GAO also suggested that data concerning work (and injuries) involving young persons were not entirely satisfactory. A more nearly adequate database was needed.[43]

Departmental initiatives, together with the investigations by GAO and the Consumers' League, combined with existing congressional concern to give the issue of child labor enhanced visibility. In early 1990, Brooks informed the Advisory Committee that a special task force on child labor would be formed within DOL and would look into such issues as possible revision of the hazardous work orders and the penalty structure for child labor violations. Brooks promised, the *Daily Labor Report* recalled, "that in the next six months, rigorous enforcement of child labor law will be the watchword of the agency."[44] Hearings followed — along with new legislative proposals. And, DOL launched *Operation Child Watch* — the first in a series of "sweeps" or general inspections aimed at compliance.[45] Changes were made in the penalty structure and, presumably, in DOL's enforcement policy.

Some viewed DOL's initiatives as a "commendable start." But there were also misgivings. Representative Don Pease (D-Ohio), one of the more outspoken advocates of child labor reform, argued that something more was needed than "occasional public relations events" and intermittent crack-downs on violators. While Pease seems to have favored legislative reform, the Bush Administration apparently did not.[46] In June 1990, Brooks assured the National Grocers Association that no new legislation was necessary: that any needed changes "can be made administratively."[47] The status of the Advisory Committee was unclear. Golodner reported in November of 1990 that no meeting of the Committee had been held since early in the year, that

---

[42] Bureau of National Affairs. *Daily Labor Report,* July 31, 1989. p. A6-A7; and August 30, 1989. p. A7-A8.

[43] Bureau of National Affairs. *Daily Labor Report, November 22,* 1989. p. A7-A8.

[44] Bureau of National Affairs. *Daily Labor Report,* February 8, 1990. p. A10-A12.

[45] Bureau of National Affairs. *Daily Labor Report,* March 19, 1990. p. A16-A17, May 1, 1990. p. A11; and June 26, 1990. p. A8-A9.

[46] Bureau of National Affairs. *Daily Labor Report,* May 4, 1990. p. A13-A15.

[47] Bureau *of* National Affairs. *Daily Labor Report,* June 25, 1990. p. A8.

the terms of current members had expired in March, and that no new members had been named by DOL. In late 1990, Secretary Dole indicated her intent to retire. Brooks resigned to return to General Motors.[48]

In 1994, the Clinton Administration proposed a general review of child labor regulation, similar in scope to that proposed by Secretary Donovan — though of a different thrust. Comprehensive oversight and administrative reform continued to be discussed but, essentially, both Congress and DOL proceeded on an *ad hoc* basis.

The "Bat Boy" Issue

In April 1986, Senator Dan Quayle (R-Ind.) proposed that child labor law be loosened to permit 14 and 15 year olds to work as bat boys or bat girls for professional baseball teams — even when games might run until late at night The Senator stated that baseball "is the All-American sport" and indicated that youngsters should not be forced to wait until they were 16 years of age "to associate with the players of their home town teams."[49] Congress mandated a study of the question — and the issue was allowed to die.

In the spring of 1993, the matter was raised again when it prevented a 14 year old youngster from Georgia from serving as a bat boy for the Savannah Cardinals. Labor Secretary Robert Reich, faced with the difficulty of explaining the logic of the work hours requirement, suspended its enforcement and proposed regulatory reform: that 14 and 15 year olds be allowed to work as late as circumstances might dictate, "before, during, and after a sporting event," around the playing field, "club house or locker room," to provide "sports-attending services at professional sporting events." Certain conditions were specified, intended to protect children from hazardous activity. And thus, by the spring of 1995, the regulation had been changed.[50]

But questions remained. For example, if it were inappropriate, *per se*, for young persons (14 and 15 years of age) to work late hours on a school night, did it really matter what sort of work they were doing? How did "sports-attending services" differ, in that context, from work in the food

---

[48] Bureau of National Affairs. *Daily Labor Report*, November 5, 1990. p. A6-A7; and November 13, 1990. p. A6.

[49] *Congressional Record*, April 9, 1986. p. S9013.

[50] *Federal Register*, May 13, 1994. p. 25167; and April 17, 1995. p. 19336-19337. The basis for the decision is explained by Robert B. Reich in his account, *Locked in the Cabinet*. New York, Alfred A. Knopf, 1997. p. 113-116.

services industry — or in a real estate or law office entering data into a computer? Might a more routine business environment be preferable to that of professional sports for the education and welfare of 14 and 15 year olds? Some in "the restaurant industry" argued that "it was unfair to exempt the sports industry from the hours and time restrictions while leaving the restrictions in place for all other employment."[51]

Paper Balers and Compactors

Under Hazardous Occupations Order No. 12, persons under 18 were not allowed to load waste paper and boxes into commercial (industrial) paper balers and compactors. Operation of such equipment, DOL had determined, was especially hazardous for younger workers. Even loading them was viewed by the Department as a serious risk. Karen Keesling, Acting Administrator of DOL's Wage and Hour Division, explained that it was not just the loading but that individuals involved in that process would likely reach into a baler or compactor to keep the materials from falling out or to clear jammed materials — and "that is extremely hazardous."[52] Conversely, the National Grocers Association termed HO 12 "a prime example of regulatory excess."[53]

In March 1995, Representative Thomas Ewing (R-Ill.) introduced H.R. 1114, legislation that would have permitted operation of the baling/compacting machinery by "minors under 18 years of age" — so long as the equipment met safety standards established by the private sector American National Standards Institute (ANSI). A similar proposal was introduced by Senator Larry Craig (R-Ida.). The legislation was supported by the National Grocers Association and opposed by the Child Labor Coalition (a youth advocacy group) and by people in the trade union movement. As signed into law (P.L. 104-174) on August 6, 1996, the legislation had been redrawn to permit workers "who are 16 and 17 years of age... to load materials into, but not operate or unload materials from, scrap paper balers and paper box compactors" that meet ANSI safety standards and where certain other requirements have been met. Whether the qualifying language

---

[51] *Federal Register,* April 17, 1995. p. 19337.

[52] Letter from Karen Keesling to Ronald A. Block (attorney for the National Grocers Association), October 16, 1992.

[53] Statement of Thomas F. Wenning, Senior Vice President and General Counsel, National Grocers Association (NGA), July 11, 1995, House Subcommittee on Workforce Protection.

was adequate to protect the youthful workers, however, remained in dispute.[54]

Work-Related Operation of Motor Vehicles

Hazardous Occupations Order No. 2, as developed at the discretion of the Secretary of Labor, restricted the work-related operation of certain motor vehicles by persons under the age of 18 as "particularly hazardous" for younger workers. While not absolutely precluded, strict guidelines and limitations had to be complied with. Conformity with specified safety standards and operation only during daylight hours was required. Employment-related driving could only be "occasional and incidental" though there might be some doubt about the definition of such terms.

In April 1994, Representative Mike Kreidler (D-Wash.) introduced legislation directing the Secretary to modify HO 2 to permit a wider opportunity for young persons to drive in conjunction with their regular work. No action was taken on the Kreidler bill and in July 1995, new legislation was introduced by Representative Randy Tate (R-Wash.) and Senator Slade Gorton (R-Wash.).Hearings followed but the legislation died at the close of the 104th Congress. In July 1997, Representative Larry Combest (R-Texas) reintroduced the issue as H.R. 2327 (the "Drive for Teen Employment Act").

Though modification of HO 2 had been endorsed by automobile dealers, it had been opposed by the Department of Labor and by groups associated with children's advocacy such as the Child Labor Coalition and the National Consumers League. Persons 16 and 17 years of age, normally, are beginning drivers who will have only recently qualified for a driver's licence. Although some youngsters may be fine drivers, it was argued that their lack of experience created a significant risk, both to the young persons themselves and to the public.

In its final form, the legislation proposed to allow persons 17 years of age to engage in limited professional driving, under specified safety conditions and with certain limitations, but would still prohibit such activity

---

[54] *Congressional Record,* May 2, 1995, p. S6009-S6010; October 24, 1995, p. H10661-H10667; and July 16, 1996, S7912-S7914. See also U.S. Congress. House. Committee on Economic and Educational Opportunities. Report 104-278. *Authority for 16 and 17 Year Olds to Load Materials into Balers and Compactors: Report to Accompany H.R. 1114.* 104th Cong., 1st Sess. Washington, U.S. Govt. Print. Off., October 17, 1995.

by persons under 17. The Combest bill, as amended, was signed by President Clinton on October 31, 1998 (P.L. 105-334).[55]

---

[55] CRS Report 98-561, *Child Labor in Hazardous Occupations: "On-the-Job Driving"* by Youth Workers, by William G. Whittaker.

CHILD LABOR INITIATIVES
DURING THE 107TH CONGRESS

Child labor concerns have, generally, been a mixture of economics and of social policy. Although Congress and DOL have resolved (at least for now) certain aspects of child labor regulation, other and often broader issues remain (see **Table 5**).

THE TRAVELING SALES CREW PROTECTION ACT

Periodically through recent years, concerns have been raised about the welfare of young persons (the age varies) who are engaged in types of outside sales work. On occasion, the focus has been upon the "street trades" — selling newspapers, candy, or other items at subway stops or, locally, from door-to-door. In such cases, a manager/supervisor may recruit young persons, move them to various local sites and, at day's end, collect them and bring them back to their homes. But, there is also another arrangement: the "traveling sales crews" in which a sales team goes on the road and remains away from its home base — overnight and possibly for extended periods. It is the latter arrangement that is addressed in legislation proposed by Senator Herb Kohl (D-Wisc.) and Representative Thomas Petri (R-Wisc.): respectively, S. 96 (and S. 2549) and H.R. 3070.

The legislative proposals suggest a number of questions. For example, how young is *too young* for children to be engaged in street sales, potentially in rough neighborhoods with which they may not be familiar? And, if they do engage in such work, through what hours should they be employed: i.e., how early in the morning and how late at night?

Table 5. Child Labor Proposals of the 107th Congress

Bill no.	Sponsor	Action beyond referral	Impact
H.R. 961	Lantos	—	Umbrella bill strengthening U.S. child labor law
H.R. 1869	Frost	—	Bill to protect young persons employed in firm also employing person with record of crime or of violence
H.R. 2239 (see S. 869)[a]	Roybal-Allard	—	The CARE Act of 2001: strengthens U.S. child labor law, special provisions dealing with children in agriculture[a]
H.R. 2639 (see S. 1241)	Pitts	—	To permit Amish youth, at age 14, to work in wood processing plants
H.R. 3070 (see S. 96)[b]	Petri	—	To provide regulations governing traveling sales crews and to prohibit employment of persons under 18 years of age in traveling sales work, under specified conditions[b]
S. 96 (see H.R. 3070)[b]	Kohl	—	Would provide new protections for young persons engaged in sales work and prohibit employment by persons under 18 years of age in traveling sales work under specified conditions[b]
S. 869 (see H.R. 2239)[a]	Harkin	—	The CARE Act of 2001 : strengthens U.S. child labor law, special provisions dealing with children in agriculture[a]
S. 1241 (see H.R. 2639)	Specter	—	To permit Amish youth, at age 14, to work in wood processing plants
S. 2549	Kohl	—	More limited than S. 96, but still governing employment of persons under 18 years of age with traveling sales crews

[a] H.R. 2239 and S. 869 are, in part, similar. H.R. 2239, however, also deals with subject matter not included in S. 869.
[b] While H.R. 3070 and S. 96 deal with the same subject area, they are structured somewhat differently and are not identical bills.

The situation becomes more complicated when groups of recruits are transported from their homes to a distant city to engage in such sales work. Are the vehicles in which they are transported safe and insured? How/where are these workers housed? Does the manager/supervisor have authority and responsibility with respect to the off-hours behavior of these young workers? What happens if one of these young persons becomes ill and needs medical attention?

Beyond the personal, there are strictly workplace questions. What is the employment relationship between these workers and the manager/supervisor? Are the youth workers employees, independent contractors, or something else entirely? To the extent that they are *employees,* by whom are they employed? The manager/supervisor may, himself, be an *employee* of some more distant entity. Where does responsibility ultimately reside? How are wages and benefits handled? What employment records are maintained — and by whom?

From a policy perspective, one might ask: Should young persons be excluded, by law, from working in street or door-to-door sales — or in related support services other than actual selling? Were otherwise applicable hours restrictions to be observed, would such work be acceptable? Would a blanket prohibition on outside sales work by persons under 18 years of age unduly restrict their capacity to earn? Is there something inherently inappropriate about street sales and/or door-to-door sales? Is such work *wrong* when 16 and 17 year olds are involved but a legitimate entrepreneurial activity if all of the sales staff (and, perhaps, support staff) are over 18? Is such work acceptable when confined to a certain radius from the permanent residence of the sales staff? And, how expansive should that radius be?

In May 1985, Representative Ron Wyden (D-Ore.), stating that "unscrupulous door-to-door selling groups" were exploiting young persons (some of them, children; others, young adults), introduced legislation to establish a National Clearinghouse on Fraudulent Youth Employment Practices. While Wyden conceded that "the vast majority of door-to-door sellers are wholly honorable and reputable," others, he suggested, were not. These companies "can be peddling anything from magazine subscriptions to chemical cleaners." He outlined a host of alleged violations of law and fraudulent sales practices engaged in by such firms and urged his colleagues to help "put these dangerous and unscrupulous operators out of business. And... take a step toward protecting our youth from dangerous employment practices."[56]

Hearings were conducted in November 1985 by the House Subcommittee on Civil and Constitutional Rights. Susan Meisinger, spokesperson for the Reagan Labor Department, testified that there was indeed a problem. "Unlawful practices reported by the States include violations of their child labor laws, violations of minimum wage laws, employer failure to pay taxes and unemployment insurance, and abuse of

---

[56] *Congressional Record*, May 16, 1985. p. E2251.

child workers," Meisinger noted, "including forcing them to pay kickbacks, child molesting, and placing them in high risk, late night employment environments."[57] Victoria Toensing, representing the Department of Justice, agreed that "problems relating to the recruitment and use of salespersons do exist" but she suggested that any legislative action would be premature. "The extent of these problems has not yet been established," Toensing stated, and, in any case, state and local authorities "may be as effective, if not more so, than the federal government in preventing such abuses." Further, she suggested, not all of the alleged worker/victims were minors. After reviewing a series of federal statutes that might apply if there actually were a problem, Toensing noted that the Department of Justice "...considers present statutory provisions adequate."[58] The Wyden bill (H.R. 2544) died at the close of the 99th Congress.

Hearings on the general issue were subsequently conducted by the Senate Permanent Subcommittee on Investigations (1987)[59] and by the House Committee on Government Operations' Subcommittee on Employment and Housing (1990).[60] In each case, the matter was restricted to general oversight. Further legislation was not then proposed.[61]

On November 19, 1999 (the 106th Congress), Senator Kohl introduced S. 1989, the "Traveling Sales Crew Protection Act" — his interest sparked by an auto accident in Wisconsin in which seven young people were killed and others injured. The Senator explained: "The driver [in the Wisconsin case] had a suspended license and a series of violations." These firms, he stated, "employ crews who travel from city to city selling products door to door. Often times," he asserted, "...[they] mistreat their workers and violate local, state, and federal labor law. Because they rapidly move from state to state, enforcement efforts are difficult if not impossible for local authorities." Senator Kohl recalled that it had been 12 years since the hearing by the

---

[57] Statement of Susan R. Meisinger, Deputy Under Secretary for Employment Standards, DOL, November 6, 1985, the House Judiciary Subcommittee on Civil and Constitutional Rights.

[58] Statement of Victoria Toensing, Deputy Assistant Attorney General, Criminal Division, November 6, 1985, the House Judiciary Subcommittee on Civil and Constitutional Rights.

[59] U.S. Congress. Senate. Committee on Governmental Affairs. Permanent Subcommittee on Investigations. Hearing. *Exploitation of Young Adults in Door-to-Door Sales.* 100th Cong., 1st Sess., April 6, 1987. 217 p.

[60] U.S. Congress. House. Committee on Government Operations. Subcommittee on Employment and Housing. Hearing. *Children at Risk in the Workplace.* 101st Cong., 2nd Sess., March 16, June 8, 1990. p. 277-297.

[61] The issue, however defined, continued to arise periodically. See: Naughton, Jim. Children's Candy Sales Are Criticized: Distributors Under Scrutiny for Possible Child Labor Infractions. *The Washington Post*, May 9, 1990. p. A1, A10; State Trying To Close Down Firm Employing Youngsters. *The Daily Olympian*, October 15, 1990. p. C1-C2; and Barrett, Julie. Kiddie Hawkers. *Generation Next,* July/August 1995. p. 22-23.

Permanent Subcommittee on Investigations and affirmed: "...nothing has changed. These abuses continue, and Congress should act."[62] But no action was taken on the bill which died at the close of the 106th Congress.

Early in the 107th Congress, Senator Kohl introduced new legislation to deal with this issue (S. 96). The Kohl bill would amend the FLSA to provide that "No individual under 18 years of age may be employed in a position requiring the individual to engage in door to door sales or in related support work in a manner that requires the individual to remain away from his or her permanent resident for more than 24 hours." After defining the operative language, the bill sets forth a registration requirement for employers and supervisors of traveling sales crew workers. Then, where such practices are allowed, it sets out the obligations of the parties — dealing with such items as housing, transportation, wages (and deductions therefrom), insurance, etc. It then lays out a system for enforcement.

On October 9, 2001, Representative Thomas Petri (R-Wisc.) introduced H.R. 3070, a similarly named but somewhat different bill.[63] Subsequently, on May 22, 2002, Senator Kohl introduced a briefer version of his own proposed legislation (S. 2549). No action has been taken on these bills.

SAWMILL WORK BY 14 YEAR OLDS

Work in or around sawmills and wood-working machinery has been deemed by DOL as especially hazardous for young persons under 18 years of age. The practice violates at least two DOL Hazardous Occupations Orders: HO 4, covering sawmills, and HO 5, dealing with power-driven wood working machines.[64]

The Amish of Pennsylvania (and of other states) resist requirements of law that would alter their traditional way of life. Many Amish avoid modem conveniences and have rejected compulsory school attendance beyond the 8th grade. The *Daily Labor Report* explains: "After completing their formal classroom training at age 14 or 15, Amish boys typically receive training in farming or carpentry from their fathers."[65] The declining opportunity to farm

---

[62] *Congressional Record*, November 19, 1999. p. S15102.

[63] *Congressional Record,* January 22, 2001. p. S361-S365.

[64] See 29 CFR 570.54 and 750.55. In a letter of July 22, 1998, to Chairman William F. Goodling (R-Pa.), Chair of the Committee on Education and the Workforce, Deputy Secretary of Labor Kathryn Higgins explained the special hazards associated with work in the lumber and wood products industry which, she said, were "exacerbated for youth" given their "lack of training" and "immaturity."

[65] Bureau of National Affairs. *Daily Labor Report*, July 23, 1998. p. A11.

(in part, because of increased land values) has led the Amish to have their children work in sawmills and wood-working plants — and, thus, to a clash with DOL over implementation of HO 4 and HO 5.

In the 105th and 106th Congresses, legislation was introduced both in the House and in the Senate that would, under specified conditions, have widened the opportunity for youth aged 14 to 18 "to be employed inside or outside places of business where machinery is used to process wood products." The bills were sponsored, respectively, by Representative Joseph R. Pitts (R-Pa.) and Senator Arlen Specter (R-Pa.). One qualification would have been that the youth "is a member of a religious sect or division thereof whose established teachings do not permit formal education beyond the eighth grade." In each Congress, the Amish legislation was passed by the House under suspension but the Senate did not act.[66]

In effect, were the legislation to be adopted, Amish children, having left school after the 8th grade, could have been employed in work otherwise regarded as too hazardous for persons under 18. Some have suggested that constitutional issues might be raised by affording special treatment to members of one religious group that are not afforded to others. Setting aside issues of legality, other questions could be raised in the context of the proposed legislation, given state policy of allowing Amish youngsters to leave school after the 8th grade. *First.* Does elimination of federal restrictions upon child labor (to the extent proposed in the legislation) provide an opportunity (and, perhaps, an incentive) for Amish children to leave school and to enter the world of work? (One might argue that they would be out of school in any case and may as well be employed.) *Second.* Assuming that these children do leave school to work, are sawmills/wood processing establishments appropriate places of employment for any youngsters under the age of 18?

In order to strengthen the ties of Amish children to the Amish community, they are systematically separated from the non-Amish world.[67] The work experience and skills which they are afforded at home on the farm

---

[66] *Congressional Record*, September 28, 1998. p. H9121-H9124. See also: U.S. Congress. House. Committee on Education and the Workforce. Subcommittee on Workforce Protections. *The Effect of the Fair Labor Standards Act on Amish Families and H.R. 2038, the MSPA Clarification Act.* Hearing. 105th Cong., 2nd Sess., April 21, 1998. Washington, U.S. Govt. Print. Off., 1998; and, U.S. Congress. House. Committee on Education and the Workforce. *Amending the Fair Labor Standards Act of 1938 To Permit Certain Youth To Perform Certain Work with Wood Products, Report Together with Minority Views To Accompany H.R. 221.* H.Rept. 106-31, 106th Cong., 1st Sess. Washington, U.S. Govt. Print. Off., 1999. 29 p.

[67] Brown, Jennifer. Old Ways Persevere, Flourish: Non-Mainstream Culture Helps Anabaptist Communities Retain Hold on the Young. *The Washington Post,* April 21, 2001. p. B9.

may not be readily transferable to the non-Amish marketplace. Thus, with only an 8th grade education and lacking experience in the non-Amish world, the choices of Amish youth may, accordingly, be restricted, rendering their out-migration from the community within which they were raised extremely difficult. Some may applaud this result; others may question the appropriateness of a federal role in its facilitation.

Since Amish children are permitted to leave school at 14 years of age, their subsequent activity may become a federal policy issue. Should they be permitted/required to work and, if so, at what types of tasks? What types of work are suitable for such children — and who should decide? As directed under the current law, DOL has reviewed the conditions of work in sawmills and woodworking facilities and has deemed such activity particularly hazardous for any youth under 18 (HO 4 and HO 5).[68]

On May 3, 2001, the Senate Appropriations Committee, Subcommittee on Labor, Health and Human Services, and Education, conducted an oversight hearing on the employment needs of Amish youth. Representative Mark Souder (R-Ind.) spoke in support of the exemption. Mr. Souder, representing a partly Amish constituency, explained that those who favor industrial work by children 14 years old had not been able to persuade DOL to acquiesce in the practice. Urging a change in the law, he argued that the Amish children would be "supervised by adults who know and care about them" and that the proposed amendment to the FLSA "would protect a truly endangered religion and culture."[69]

Thomas M. Markey, Acting Administrator of the Wage and Hour Division, DOL, also testified concerning employment of Amish youth. He stated that, for reasons of their faith, Amish youth "are exempt from state laws making school attendance compulsory" and, when they have finished the 8th grade and are 14 years old, they are permitted to work more hours than would normally be the case "and to work during traditional school hours." However, he pointed out: "Sawmills are dangerous places to work, even for adults." Pointing to a high accident and fatality rate for the industry nationwide, he stated that such work is "even more dangerous for children."[70]

---

[68] This is a *work opportunity* (or *endangerment*) that would not apply with respect to children who are of religious denominations other than Amish and/or certain closely related sects.

[69] Testimony of Representative Mark Souder before the Senate Subcommittee on Labor, Health and Human Services and Education, Committee on Appropriations, May 3, 2001.

[70] Testimony of Thomas M. Markey, Acting Administrator, Wage and Hour Division, U.S. Department of Labor, before the Subcommittee on Labor, Health and Human Services, and Education, Committee on Appropriations, U.S. Senate, May 3, 2001.

On June 13, 2001, during consideration of S. 1 (reauthorization of the Elementary and Secondary Education Act), Senator Specter proposed S.Amdt. 420. The Specter amendment would have amended the FLSA to permit Amish youngsters who are over 14 and exempt from compulsory school attendance to work, under specified conditions, in wood products processing. Following an opening statement, a brief colloquy was engaged in between Senators Specter and Edward M. Kennedy (D-Mass.) — the latter chair, Committee on Health, Education, Labor, and Pensions. Senator Kennedy affirmed that it "would be valuable to have... an open hearing" on the issue — particularly with respect to the safety of prospective workers — and agreed that the Committee would conduct such a hearing. At that point, Senator Specter withdrew his proposed amendment, awaiting opportunity for a further hearing on industrial employment of Amish youth.[71]

On July 25, 2001, legislation to permit Amish youth to work at age 14 in wood processing plants was introduced both in the House and in the Senate: H.R. 2639 (Pitts) and S. 1241 (Specter). No action has been taken on these proposals beyond referral to committee.

THE "CARE" ACT OF 2001

Except where plantations predominated, early agriculture in America focused upon the family farm: a small operation run by a single family with, perhaps, one or two hired hands. In that context, children worked alongside parents who, presumably, watched over them and cared for them. Thus, early initiatives with respect to regulation of child labor encountered opposition from family farmers who feared that such regulation would intrude upon their ability to employ their own children on their own *family* farms.[72] That concern appears to have been one of the impediments to approval of the

---

[71] *Congressional Record*, June 13, 2001. p. S6153-S6154.

[72] Viviana A. Zelizer, in her study, *Pricing the Priceless Child: The Changing Social Value of Children*. Princeton, Princeton University Press, 1994, p. 77, points to a differentiation between agricultural labor and industrial labor where children were concerned. "If defending factory work was unusual, farm labor on the other hand was almost blindly and romantically categorized as 'good' work." And, work, however harsh, supervised by a parent was also regarded as *good* work, she suggests. From the *American Review of Reviews* from 1924 (p. 79), by way of example, she quotes: "'Work on the farm performed by children under parents' direction and without interference with school attendance is not child labor. Work performed by children away from home, for wages, at long hours and under conditions which endanger the child's health, education and morals is child labor.'" That philosophy was largely written into the FLSA in 1938.

child labor constitutional amendment (1924 ff).[73] Thus, under the FLSA, children engaged in agricultural work have been treated differently from those in non-agricultural occupations and a family farm (child labor) exemption is specifically a part of the statute.

Through the years, the family farm has given way to larger holdings and to agribusiness: that is to say, corporate agriculture with hundreds of workers. Concern with agricultural labor by children has similarly shifted. The child, engaged in agriculture, may now often be a son or daughter of migrant or local seasonal agricultural workers. He may be individually *employed* or may work as part of a family group. He may also be an informal employee: off the books and not officially employed but working nonetheless. Through it all, though the FLSA has been modified in a variety of respects and agricultural employment has come increasingly under the wage and hour standards of the Act, agricultural child labor continues to be treated differently from non-agricultural child labor. While the former may no longer be idealized, it may have become nearly invisible.

In the 107th Congress, at least two bills have been introduced that deal with the regulation of child labor in agriculture. Though they are not identical (and, in some respects, quite different), each carries the title: the "Children's Act for Responsible Employment of 2001" or the "CARE Act." Neither has been acted upon.

The Harkin "CARE" Act

On May 10, 2001, Senator Tom Harkin (D-Iowa) introduced S. 869, which was referred to the Committee on Health, Education, Labor, and Pensions. The Harkin bill begins with a reaffirmation that children "employed in agriculture outside of school hours," if employed by a parent or other close relative, will not be subject to the child labor provisions (Section 12) of the FLSA. It would not alter current practice where children work with their parent (or close family member) on that individual's own farm.

The bill then strikes two provisions of existing law. (a) It would remove the distinction between children employed in agricultural and in non-agricultural work with respect to types of work the Secretary has found to be "particularly hazardous" for persons under 18. For such hazardous work, 18 years of age would be the floor, younger persons being barred. (b) It would

---

[73] McQuade, *The American Catholic Attitude,* op. cit., p. 125.

repeal the 1977 provision of the FLSA (Section 13(c)(4)) that would, otherwise, permit employment of children between 10 and 12 in field harvest work where there is, demonstrably, no hazard from pesticide or related toxins. Employment of 10 and 12 year olds in commercial agriculture would not be permitted.

In addition, the Harkin bill would make a number of administration and compliance changes. It would restructure the civil and criminal penalties for child labor law violations at large. It directs the Secretary of Labor and the Director of the Bureau of the Census to compile, biannually, data concerning (a) the types of industries and occupations in which children under 18 are employed and (b) the cases in which children were employed in violation of FLSA child labor provisions. The bill would also require certain reports by employers of persons under 18. Finally, the Secretaries of Labor and Health and Human Services would be required to issue a biannual report on the status of child labor in the United States "and its attendant safety and health hazards."

The Roybal-Allard "CARE" Act

On June 19, 2001, Representative Lucille Roybal-Allard (D-Calif.) introduced H.R. 2239 which was referred to the Committee on Education and the Workforce and to the Committee on Agriculture. With some variations in language, H.R. 2239 incorporates the substance of S. 869.

The Roybal-Allard bill, however, has provisions that go beyond those of the Harkin bill. *First.* H.R. 2239 calls for employment of "at least 100 additional inspectors within the Wage and Hour Division" of DOL "for the principal purpose of enforcing compliance with child labor laws." It also calls for a 10% increase in the budget of the Solicitor of Labor for prosecution of child labor law violations. *Second.* The federal Insecticide, Fungicide, and Rodenticide Act would be amended to mandate development of special standards with respect to pesticide use where children and pregnant or nursing women are present (near) or employed. It would require a review of such standards every 5 years, promulgation of specific requirements for the conduct of pesticide-related inspections, and annual publication of the "findings and results of such inspections for each State." *Third.* The Workforce Investment Act of 1998 would be amended to provide a new "Migrant and Seasonal Farmworker Youth Dropout Prevention" program designed to strengthen and expand educational and training opportunities for migratory youth.

YOUNG AMERICAN WORKERS' BILL OF RIGHTS

In 1990 (the 101st Congress), Representatives Don Pease (D-Ohio), Charles Schumer (D-N. Y.) and Tom Lantos (D-Calif .) — with 37 co-sponsors — introduced legislation titled the "Young American Workers' Bill of Rights." With various changes (but with a continuity of thrust), the legislation has been reintroduced in each Congress thereafter.

On March 8, 2001 (with many of the original co-sponsors still in support), Representative Lantos introduced H.R. 961, the current edition of the proposal. The Lantos bill is comprehensive. *Inter alia:*

a) It requires the Secretary of Labor and the United States Census Bureau to compile data on the extent and nature of child labor in America, including an inventory of work-related injuries or illnesses involving child workers.

b) It redefines "minor" to include "an individual who is under the age of 18 and who has not received a high school diploma or its equivalent or who is 18 and enrolled full-time in a high school." Such minors may not be employed in the absence of "a valid certificate of employment" issued by "a State agency." It sets forth in detail the conditions to be satisfied prior to issuance of such certificates of employability.[74]

c) It directs the Secretary of Labor to revise the existing system of hazardous occupation orders (HO's), listing types of work unsuitable by reason of their hazardous character for persons under a specified age.

d) It directs the Secretary, through regulation, to prohibit "individuals under 16" years of age "from making door-to-door sales for profit."

e) Through regulation, "individuals under 16" would be "prohibited from using fryers, baking equipment, and cooking equipment in food service establishments" including "soda fountains, lunch counters, snack bars, or cafeteria serving counters."

---

[74] Linking school attendance and/or achievement with youth employment certification has been attempted in other contexts but, while the concept may be appealing, it has sometimes proven difficult to administer and may impose responsibilities for which "a State agency" and the school system may not be prepared. See also item (i).

f)   The Secretary of Labor is directed to establish an Advisory Committee for Child Labor to be composed of "not less than 21 individuals, and shall include representatives of government, labor, industry, education, agriculture, health professions, small business, youth, service industries, retailers, consumer interests, human rights, child welfare, parent groups, and the general public." The structure, functions, etc., of the Committee are specified.

g)   It revises the penalty structure for child labor violations — both for Criminal and civil penalties.

h)   It mandates "closer working relationships among Federal and State agencies having responsibility for enforcing labor, safety and health, and immigration laws."

i)   It affirms that: "The Secretary of Labor shall publish and disseminate the names and addresses of each person who has willfully violated the provisions of Section 12 of the Fair Labor Standards Act of 1938 relating to child labor or any regulation under such section and the types of violations committed by such person and shall distribute the publication regionally." The names of employers who violate federal child labor law will be made "available to affected school districts."

j)   It eliminates any small business exemption from the amended statute.

k)   It defines as oppressive child labor employment of any person "under the age of 14... as a migrant agricultural worker... or seasonal agricultural worker."

The bill was referred to the Committee on Education and the Workforce, Subcommittee on Workforce Protections. No further action has been taken.

TO PROTECT YOUTH WORKERS FROM SOCIAL HARM

On May 16, 2001, Representative Martin Frost (D-Texas) introduced the "Amy Robinson Memorial Act," H.R. 1869, which would amend the FLSA by adding a new Section 14(e)(1).

H.R. 1869 is designed to assure that a parent or guardian is given "prompt written notice" in cases in which a youth is employed in association with a fellow worker who has a history of violent crime. It directs the Secretary of Labor to provide such notice where (a) the employee is under 18 years of age or employed under DOL certification in a sheltered work environment, (b) the employer "knows or reasonably should know that the earning or productive capacity of the employee is impaired by physical or mental deficiency, or injury," (c) another individual with "a criminal record that includes a conviction for a crime of violence... performs work at the same facility as the employee," and (d) the employer "employs the other individual" and "knows or reasonably should know of the conviction." The notice to the parent or guardian of the youth or disabled worker "shall contain an identification of the facility, a statement that an individual who had been convicted of a crime of violence performs work at the facility, and an identification of each such crime of violence."

In a news release, Representative Frost explained that Amy Robinson, late of Arlington, Texas, a "mentally challenged women... was murdered by a co-worker in 1998." He stated that he was introducing the legislation (identical to a bill he had introduced in the 106ᵗʰ Congress) to ensure "that parents receive written notice if their child starts a new job where they will be working with a violent felon."[75]

The bill was referred to the Committee on Education and the Workforce, Subcommittee on Workforce Protections. No further action has been taken.

---

[75] Press release from the office of Representative Martin Front, May 17, 2001.

INDEX